THE BIG BOOK OF REAL BOATS AND SHIPS

COAST GUARD CUTTER • Along the coasts of our country, small, fast vessels called Coast Guard cutters travel back and forth all the time. When a cutter's radio picks up the letters S O S, the international signal of distress, she knows that a ship is in trouble, and she rushes to help. If the ship is sinking, Coast Guardsmen try to save the lives of the passengers and seamen.

In this picture a freighter is going down, and a cutter is shooting out a lifeline. The men on the freighter will catch the line and tie it to her mast. Then, one by one, they will slide over to the cutter, in a little chair which will be hung from the lifeline.

Coast Guardsmen also send out radio signals which help to guide airplanes flying over the ocean. They send radio reports about the weather. And they're always on the watch for smugglers, too!

THE BIG BOOK OF REAL BOATS AND SHIPS

ANY LARGE, SEAGOING VESSEL IS A SHIP. BUT A SMALL, OPEN
VESSEL MOVED BY OARS, PADDLES, SAILS OR MOTOR IS A BOAT.

By GEORGE J. ZAFFO

ISBN: 0-448-02254-0 (TRADE EDITION)

ISBN: 0-448-03728-9 (LIBRARY EDITION)

GROSSET & DUNLAP   Publishers   NEW YORK
1976 Printing
COPYRIGHT, 1951, BY GROSSET & DUNLAP, INC.
LITHOGRAPHED IN THE UNITED STATES OF AMERICA

TUGBOAT • Big ships are too clumsy to go alone into or out of their places alongside piers. They need small boats to help them. Tugboats do this work. They can nose their padded bows against a ship and push very hard. They can pull very hard, too. They often pull whole strings of flat-bottomed boats, called barges, carrying heavy loads of coal, sand, or even railroad cars.

Seagoing tugs are big and strong enough to travel over the ocean. Other tugs

are built very low so that they can pull canal barges under bridges. The tug shown here is a harbor tug. It has a crew of seven men. The captain is in charge. The mate helps him. A deckhand takes care of the tug's big ropes. The chief engineer has charge of the engines. The oiler oils them and keeps the engine room clean. The fireman feeds the engines fuel. And, of course, there is a cook who makes chow for the whole crew.

SUBMARINE • The nuclear-powered attack submarine shown here is the U.S.S. "Skipjack." A true submarine, the "Skipjack" can go all around the world under water. It can travel over 100,000 miles before it needs refueling. Some nuclear subs can dive to a depth of over 400 feet and some can fire missiles while under the surface. Officers and sailors have stayed aboard under water for as long as 83 days before returning to the surface.

This is how a sub dives: She has tanks which can be filled with air or water. When there is air in the tanks, she floats on the surface. When there is water in the tanks, she becomes too heavy to float, so she goes down under the surface. The hydro-wings on the fin (the fin was once called the conning tower) and the stern (rear) control planes are used like the controls on an airplane. To see on the surface while under water, a sub uses a periscope.

THE FIRST BOAT. Nobody knows what the first boat in the world looked like. But we can guess that people began to travel across water by holding onto a log and paddling with one arm.

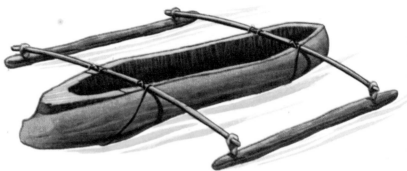

OUTRIGGER. We do know that long, long ago, men discovered they could get around better if they hollowed out a log and sat inside. To keep the "boat" from tipping over, they sometimes fastened smaller logs on each side. Boats with these balancers are still used. They are called outriggers.

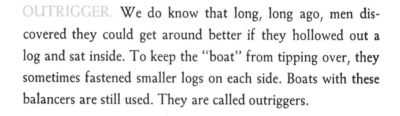

VIKING SHIP. Still later, men discovered how useful oars can be. And then they found out about sails. Here is a Viking long ship that has both oars and a sail. The Vikings were fearless seamen, and they sailed across the Atlantic Ocean even before Columbus did.

"SANTA MARIA." By the time Columbus came, men knew that ships could travel without oars if they had enough sails, and could carry cargo, too. Here is the "Santa Maria," one of the three boats in which Columbus and his men sailed.

"CLERMONT." This is the first steamboat, which Robert Fulton built and ran up the Hudson River from New York to Albany. People along the banks ran away in fright when they saw the noisy, smoky vessel coming along without sails.

"MAYFLOWER." Sailing ships became bigger and bigger as men learned more about building them. This is the famous ship which brought the Pilgrims to America.

AMERICAN CLIPPER. Even after steamboats were invented, men kept on making faster and better sailing ships. American clipper ships like the "Rainbow," shown here, were the fastest of all, and they won many races, sailing halfway around the world, carrying valuable cargoes.

IRONCLAD WARSHIPS. These two warships were made of wood covered with iron. They fought one of the famous sea battles of the Civil War. The "Monitor," flying the American flag, was nicknamed a "cheese box on a raft." She defeated the "Merrimac," which belonged to the South.

CARGO VESSEL • Ships that carry heavy loads of freight are called cargo vessels or freighters. If you know a lot about them, you can tell the different models, just as you can tell one automobile from another. The "Sea Serpent," shown here, is a C2-S-B1. The cargo is stored deep down inside the ship in big rooms called holds. Derricks on the ship, which are called booms, pick up the cargo from the pier and lower it into the holds through hatches, which are openings in the deck.

The booms are the long, slender poles sticking up and out, with ropes and pulleys dangling from them. When a freighter is at sea, these booms are tied down close to the deck so they won't swing around. Sailors call this "cradling" the booms. The big posts which hold the booms up are called king posts or Samson posts. Sometimes sailors call them goal posts, because they look like goal posts on a football field. On some freighters, masts instead of king posts hold up the booms.

WHISTLE SIGNALS

If a vessel is turning to starboard (right), it gives one short blast on its whistle.

If it is turning to port (left), a vessel gives two short blasts on its whistle.

Three short blasts mean a vessel is backing up.

Four short blasts mean "Danger!"

A vessel gives one long blast to warn other vessels that it is about to leave a pier.

When a vessel gives three long blasts, it is just saying "Hello!" to some other vessel.

A vessel blows its whistle only when it wants to give a signal to other vessels. And other vessels always show that they have heard the signal by answering with the same signal on their own whistles.

As you know, there are right-of-way rules for automobiles at crossings. The rules tell which cars have to stop and let the others go ahead first. Vessels have right-of-way rules, too. Look at the shaded part of the round picture. The vessel in the shaded part has the right of way over the vessels in the white part. Only the shaded part is a danger zone for the vessel in the center. It has the right of way over other vessels in the white part. All the other vessels have danger zones on their starboard (right) sides, too.

HOW, WHEN AND WHY THE SHIP'S BELL IS STRUCK

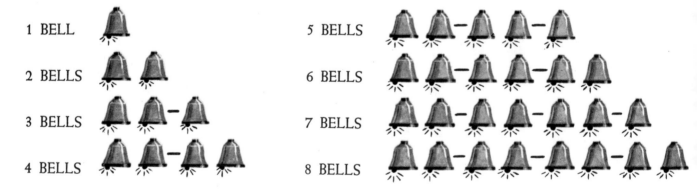

1 BELL	5 BELLS
2 BELLS	6 BELLS
3 BELLS	7 BELLS
4 BELLS	8 BELLS

Starting with three bells, the bell is struck in pairs, with a short pause before additional bells (strokes) are struck.

There are six tours of watch duty on board a vessel, each one four hours long. The first watch starts at 8:00 P.M. and ends at midnight. At 8:30, one stroke on the ship's bell indicates that the first half hour of the watch has been completed. An additional bell is struck for each succeeding half hour, so that when midnight comes, eight bells are struck. Then the next four-hour watch starts, and the bells begin all over again. One bell means 12:30 A.M., and so on, up to eight bells, which now mean it is 4 A.M.

ENGINE ROOM TELEGRAPH

The captain stands in the wheelhouse. When he wants the ship to go faster or slower, or stop, or back up, he gives the order to the chief engineer, who is way down inside the ship, in the engine room. The captain signals the engineer on the engine room telegraph.

If the captain wishes the ship to stop, he pushes the handle on his telegraph until it points to STOP. The engineer has his telegraph down in the engine room. To show

he has received the message, he pushes *his* handle to STOP. This moves the white arrow on the captain's telegraph to STOP. When the handle and the arrow are lined up, the captain knows the engineer has received his order. If the captain wants the ship to go ahead slowly, he pushes the handle to DEAD SLOW, on the left side of the telegraph. If he wants it to back up slowly, he pushes the handle to DEAD SLOW on the right.

INTERNATIONAL CODE FLAG SIGNALS

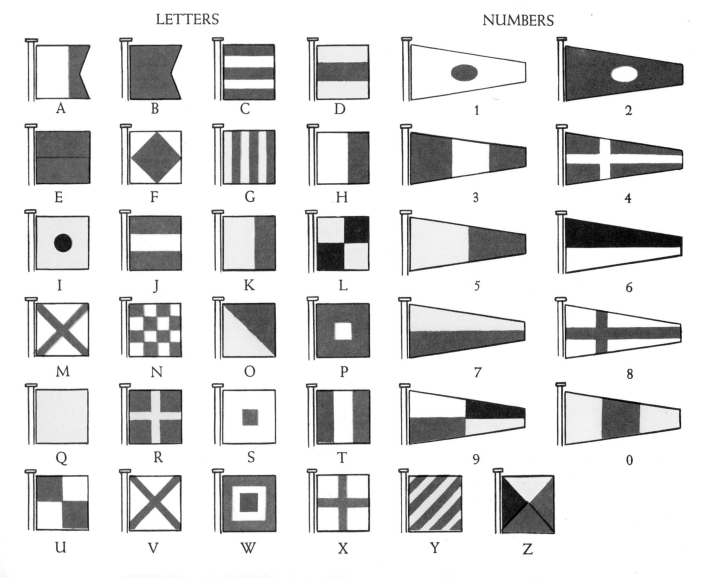

LETTERS   NUMBERS

A   B   C   D   1   2

E   F   G   H   3   4

I   J   K   L   5   6

M   N   O   P   7   8

Q   R   S   T   9   0

U   V   W   X   Y   Z

OCEAN LINER • A liner is a big ship that carries passengers. The "Queen Elizabeth" is the largest liner in the world. She is five blocks long and has fourteen decks. That means she is as high as a fourteen-story building, with elevators that take people up and down. She is really like a floating city, for thirty-five hundred people can live on her while she travels back and forth across the ocean. They eat in dining rooms as big as restaurants. They go to movies, swim in the pool, exercise in the

gym, and play games on the decks. Children have a special room to play in. There is a barbershop for the men and a beauty parlor for the women. Even the dogs have an exercise deck, all their own!

There is so much work to do on the "Queen Elizabeth" that it takes twelve hundred people to do it. There is even work for radio-telephone operators, who can connect you with any number you want to call almost anywhere in the world.

SMALL CRAFT

LIFEBOAT. If a ship is sinking, people get into lifeboats, lower them to the water, and escape. The lifeboat shown here is a motorboat. The man is holding the rudder used to steer the boat.

SAMPAN. The Chinese use sampans as small cargo boats, water taxis, and sometimes even as traveling stores.

SCULL. This is a very light boat, built to go very fast and used mostly for racing.

ROWBOAT. A rowboat is a sturdy boat rowed with oars. The small rowboat you often see being towed behind a sailing vessel or motorboat is called a dinghy.

KAYAK. An Eskimo makes his kayak of animal skin. He laces the opening tightly around his waist to keep water out.

LIFE RAFT. Many ships carry air-filled rubber rafts to which shipwrecked people can cling till help comes.

SAILING DINGHY. This is the name for a dinghy that carries a sail as well as oars.

CANOE. Indians invented the canoe, which they made of bark. Today, many canoes are made of waterproofed canvas.

OUTBOARD RACER. A noisy motor with a propeller, which is attached at the stern of this small boat, pushes the boat through the water very fast.

ODD CRAFT

HOUSEBOAT. Many people live on flat-bottomed houseboats like this one. But the boats have to be towed in order to move from place to place.

JUNK. The captain of this Chinese cargo vessel lives on board with not only his whole family, but even with his chickens and ducks.

HYDROPLANE. A propeller in the air instead of in the water makes a hydroplane go.

CATAMARAN. Gar Wood, a famous motorboat builder and racer, designed this craft, which is modeled after fast South Sea sailboats called catamarans.

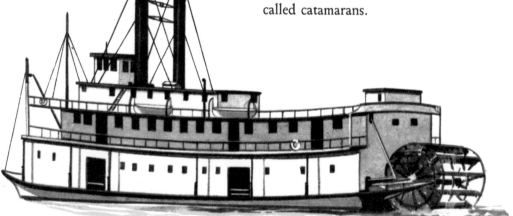

RIVER BOAT. Boats like this travel up and down the Mississippi River. Called stern-wheelers, they have a big wheel that pushes them from behind, instead of paddle wheels at the sides.

FIREBOAT • Here is the "Firefighter," the biggest fireboat in the world, trying to save a burning freighter. All her nozzles together can shoot out as much water as twenty fire engines could on land. One big nozzle in the bow squirts enough water in a minute to fill a swimming pool. The nozzle on the tower shoots farther than the others. It can aim water at the deck of the freighter or even down into the hold.

Most big seaports have at least one fireboat. New York City has ten. They

fight fires along the waterfront, when piers are burning or when vessels catch fire. They sometimes help firemen on land by pumping water to them. And they even go out to sea, where they help ships that have radioed that they are burning. Because of the dangerous machinery used, seagoing firemen cannot have mascots.

Tugboats like the one shown here near the "Firefighter" can fight fires, too. Many of them have a nozzle high up in the bow, which can be used in emergencies.

PARTS OF A DUAL-ENGINE CRUISER. This is a small dual-engine cruiser which people use mostly for fun. But the names of the parts you see here are used on all kinds of boats and ships.

1. ENSIGN
2. MOORING BITTS
3. STERN DECK
4. STERN HATCH
5. COMPANIONWAY DOOR TO AFT CABIN
6. FLYING BRIDGE DECK
7. PORT SIDE (left side)
8. STEERING WHEEL
9. CONTROL PANEL
10. 32-POINT WHITE RANGE LIGHT
11. HAND THROTTLE
12. WINDSHIELD
13. HORN
14. RED PORT SIDE LIGHT (10 points)
15. HANDRAILS
16. GREEN STARBOARD SIDE LIGHT (10 points)
17. FORWARD HATCH
18. ANCHOR
19. PENNANT
20. 20-POINT WHITE BOW RANGE LIGHT
21. BOW (front of boat)
22. PORTHOLES
23. DECKHOUSE
24. DRAFT
25. STARBOARD SIDE (right side)
26. VENTILATORS
27. CORK RING BUOYS (lifesavers)
28. AFT CABIN
29. LINE CLEATS
30. VENTILATOR
31. EXHAUST PIPES
32. PROPELLERS
33. RUDDERS
34. STERN (back of boat)

RANGE LIGHTS

At night a vessel turns on white lights which are called range lights. The front (bow) light is always lower than the rear (stern) light. Each vessel also has a red light on its left (port) side and a green light on its right (starboard) side. These are called running lights. Anyone seeing them can tell in which direction the vessel is moving.

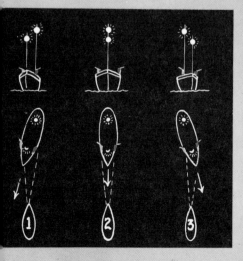

The diagram at the left shows how lights keep vessels from ramming each other at night. Imagine you are in vessel No. 1. You see both red and green lights ahead. This means a vessel is coming toward you. (Colored lights and the bow range lights are fixed so that you can't see them from behind.) Now look at the range lights. The lower or bow light is at your left. So you know the vessel is headed toward your left (port) side. Now imagine you're in vessel No. 2. You see red and green lights. The range lights are in a straight line up and down. You know the other vessel is coming straight toward you. If you are in vessel No. 3, the lower range light is to the right of the higher one. The other vessel is headed to your right (starboard) side.

⑩ ⑪ ⑫ ⑬ ⑭ ⑮ ⑯ ⑰ ⑱ ⑲ ⑳ ㉑ ㉒ ㉓ ㉔ ㉕ ㉖ ㉗

MOTOR SET-UP
IN A CABIN CRUISER

1. MOTOR   2. DRIVE SHAFT   3. PROPELLER

The skipper shifts gears to go forward or backward.

He makes the motor go as fast as he wants by using a hand throttle which gives the motor more gas. The motor turns the drive shaft, which turns the propeller. When the propeller turns in one direction, the blades push the water behind them, and that shoves the boat forward. When they turn in the other direction, they push the water ahead of them, and that makes the boat back up.

DIRECTIONS AT SEA

If a sailor standing in the center of a vessel sees another vessel straight ahead of him, he says it is *dead ahead*. If he sees a vessel way behind him on the left, he says it is on *the port quarter*. The chart at the left shows other words used to describe direction. These points also divide the lights.

White stern range light (in back) shines in all directions. It is called a 32-point light, because the compass sailors use has 32 points, or directions, marked on it.

White bow range light (in front) shines a little more than halfway around. A 20-point light, it is visible from dead ahead to two points abaft the beam on either side.

Red port side light (left) is a 10-point light. It is visible from dead ahead to two points abaft the port beam.

Green starboard side light (right) is a 10-point light, visible from dead ahead to two points abaft the starboard beam.

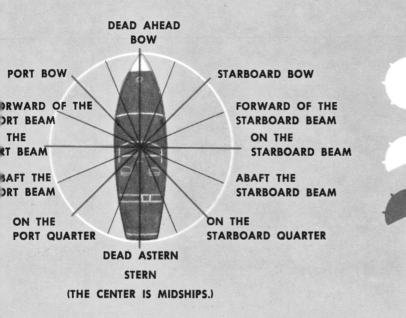

DEAD AHEAD
BOW

PORT BOW   STARBOARD BOW

ORWARD OF THE   FORWARD OF THE
RT BEAM   STARBOARD BEAM

THE   ON THE
RT BEAM   STARBOARD BEAM

AFT THE   ABAFT THE
RT BEAM   STARBOARD BEAM

ON THE   ON THE
PORT QUARTER   STARBOARD QUARTER

DEAD ASTERN
STERN
(THE CENTER IS MIDSHIPS.)

SAILBOATS • People have sailboats mainly for fun. They take cruises in them along the seacoasts or on big lakes. Sometimes they race each other, and the boats skim over the water at high speed, with nothing but the wind filling the sails to push them.

The boats in this picture are yawls. The sail over the bow of the yawl is a jib. The sail by the big mast is the mainsail, and the little one in the stern is the mizzen sail. Yawls come in different sizes, but usually they are big enough to have bunks

for people to sleep in and a galley where they can cook. There are many other kinds of sailboats, too. You can tell them apart by the types of sails they have.

The buoy at the left guides vessels near shore. It has a light at the top and four bells down below. The buoy floats on the water, though actually it is anchored in one place. Night or day, and in fog, too, vessels can tell where they are by the sight or sound of the buoys.

LIGHT SIGNALS

YACHT   OCEAN LINER   STEAM TRAWLER

Vessels of different sizes, doing different things, show different lights at night. The yacht's lights show that it is coming straight toward you. The ocean liner's lights tell you that you are looking at its port side. The trawler's lights show it is a small fishing vessel, moving, with no nets in the water.

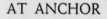

AT ANCHOR

Vessels use their red and green lights only while they are moving. When they drop their anchors, they turn these lights off and use only white ones. A small vessel at anchor turns on only one white light. A vessel more than 150 feet long turns on two. The bow light is always higher than the stern light, so that anyone can tell which end of the ship is which, even in the dark.

INLAND TUGS WITH TOW

At night, tugboats and the vessels they are towing have different arrangements of lights. These lights show how many vessels are being towed alongside a tug. Sometimes they are towed astern (behind) in a string. Or vessels may be towed astern of the tug but alongside each other.

26-FT. CRUISER

When under way, the small cruiser on the left and the larger cruiser on the right have two white lights at night. These lights

26-FT. SAIL- AND MOTORBOAT

are fixed in place. The middle picture shows a motorboat that also has a sail. This kind of boat does not have fixed lights at

42-FT. CRUISER

night, but the skipper always keeps a white lantern ready to use if he thinks he is in danger of being hit by another vessel.

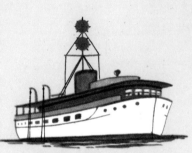

VESSELS IN DISTRESS

The lights on the vessel above show that for some reason it can't be steered—that it is "not under control," as sailors say.

This vessel, though not under control, has a white light over the bow to show that it is anchored and not just floating around.

The sailboat carries a white lantern in case of danger. Motorboats recognize a sailboat's lights and give it the right of way.

OCEAN-GOING TUG

The lights on seagoing tugs are different from those of inland tugs which work in harbors and on rivers, lakes, and canals.

AIRCRAFT CARRIER • An aircraft carrier is really an airfield that can move all around the world on the ocean. Airplanes are stored inside the carrier with their wings folded up. Elevators take the folded planes up to the top deck, called the flight deck. There, men straighten the wings out, and the planes are ready to fly.

Every airplane on the carrier has a hook near its tail. When the plane lands, this hook catches onto what is called the arresting gear, on the flight deck This stops

the plane, the way you would stop a flying bird if you caught its feet and held them tight. If a plane does fall into the water, the carrier sends out a special little boat, called a crash boat, to rescue the flier and bring him back.

The officers run the carrier from a tower, called the Island, located on the starboard side of the flight deck. Inside the carrier, the sailors have dining rooms, places to sleep, a laundry where they wash clothes, and even soda fountains.

COAST GUARD CUTTER • Along the coasts of our country, small, fast vessels called Coast Guard cutters travel back and forth all the time. When a cutter's radio picks up the letters S O S, the international signal of distress, she knows that a ship is in trouble, and she rushes to help. If the ship is sinking, Coast Guardsmen try to save the lives of the passengers and seamen.

In this picture a freighter is going down, and a cutter is shooting out a lifeline. The men on the freighter will catch the line and tie it to her mast. Then, one by one, they will slide over to the cutter, in a little chair which will be hung from the lifeline.

Coast Guardsmen also send out radio signals which help to guide airplanes flying over the ocean. They send radio reports about the weather. And they're always on the watch for smugglers, too!